TABLE OF CONTENT

How To Buy and Sell Online For A Living

CHAPTER 1

How to get started selling online

    A. Business Tool Kit
    B. Make time to learn
    C. Getting Organized
    D. Places to find products for sale in your area

CHAPTER 2

How to find profitable products online

    A. Websites that sell products for cents of the dollar
    B. Choosing your niche
    C. Knowing the value of your products
    D. Is your product in demand

CHAPTER 3

How to bid like a pro

    A. Organizing your auction times
    B. When to bid
    C. Common bidding errors
    D. When to go for the gold

CHAPTER 4

How to list your items for sale

    A. The best places to sell your product online
    B. How to write excellent descriptions
    C. Adding visuals to your listings
    D. Finding the competitive price point

CHAPTER 5

How to deliver your product to the customer

    A. How to package your item
    B. Choosing a shipping company
    C. When to insure an item
    D. Track your items

CHAPTER 6

How to provide great customer service

- A. Establishing direct contact with customers
- B. Be a problem solver
- C. Dealing with dishonest customers
- D. Getting repeat customers

CHAPTER 7

How to expand your business

- A. Choosing new products
- B. Taking out a loan
- C. Creating Partners
- D. Teaching Others

INTRODUCTION

WELCOME TO SELL FOR A LVING, WE ARE VERY GLAD YOU DECIDED TO JOIN US. IN THIS COURSE YOU WILL LEARN HOW TO CREATE A PROFITABLE BUSINESS ONLINE. IT IS OUR MISSION TO EDUCATE OUR MEMBERS AND PROMOTE A POSITIVE COMMUNITY OF BUYERS AND SELLERS ONLINE. IF YOU'RE AN ESTABLISHED BUYER OR SELLER, WE'VE GOT THE TOOLS YOU NEED TO GROW YOUR BUSINESS TO THE NEXT LEVEL. BEFORE WE DIVE INTO THE NUTS AND BOLTS OF ONLINE AUCTIONS, IF YOU DON'T ALREADY HAVE A BUSINESS TOOL KIT, YOU'RE GOING TO NEED A FEW ITEMS TO RUN YOUR ONLINE BUSINESS SUCCESSFULLY.

CHAPTER 1

SETTING UP YOUR BUSINESS TOOL KIT

So you've decided to invest in online auctions as a great source of income. You've made a wise choice, however without the right setup you could lose out of many auctions and end up frustrated and disappointed. First make sure you have a reliable computer desktop or laptop. If you have a virus on your computer get it removed. They slow down the speed of your Internet connection and that can be a disaster on some of the website with no time extension on bids. Make sure you have plenty of ram and disk space for streaming videos and downloading pictures from your phone or other media devices.

Don't underestimate the importance of a good Internet service provider. In many cases if you go with an Internet service that doesn't have a strong signal in your area you'll end up dealing with outage and poor connection speed. Ask them for their fastest Internet connection speed and if it's not much higher, it's worth it to have good speed with online auctions. We'll get into exactly why later in the course.

Notes pads are still a great way to organize. Even though you could type your information on the computer, note pads will help organize your thoughts much better than a computer will in my opinion. I use my note pad for setting goals, or writing down investment plans and for creative ideas. It's the proven way to put your vision to use. Call me old school but I believe there's something special about writing an idea down on paper that makes it real and worth achieving.

MAKE TIME TO LEARN

So you've got a good computer or laptop. The fastest and most reliable Internet Service Provider (ISP) you could find and a notepad for your ideas and goals. Next you'll need a place where you can focus without noise or distractions. If you're a mom or dad at home with the kids, find a time when you don't have to watch them as much. Most often this is after their bedtime. If you don't have a place at home then go to a library or coffee shop. You must be able to focus, you'll miss out on too many great deals simply because you're distracted and not paying enough attention to your auctions. Much of your success with online auctions will be determined by how well you find and research items. The more you research, the more money you make. I'll definitely spend some time on that subject in detail later on in this course. So make certain you have a place in mind that you can go and give all your attention to the online auctions. This is the basic business tool kit for your online auction business.

If you're new, you probably haven't set aside some time for learning. I would recommend spending at least 2 hours day to read and research products. This isn't a get rich quick method so the more time you put in, the faster you'll start earning the income you want or need. Make time for your business. How many times have you tried a business without really studying and ended up starting over with some thing totally different? We've all done it before. I want to save you some time by assuring you that if you use the strategies you earn in this ebook, you will be able to make profitable purchases. How much money you make is up to you and your work habits.

GETTING ORGANIZED

When I first started out bidding online, I was always getting beat out or forgetting the time of the auction. I'd get an email notification prior to an auction ending but by the time I got to my laptop it was almost over and I didn't feel confident in bidding. Most of the time I tried bidding, I would keep getting out bid. Or bid way too much.

Truthfully I was about to call it quits. I lost money on the first 3-4 auctions because my research was poor and I didn't know how calculate all the cost versus selling price (more on this later). Then I pulled out my trusty notepad and started writing down the auctions I missed and calculating how much profit I missed out on. When I figured out how much I was losing, I knew I had to do something about it. I knew that if I could win I'd get to make the profit. In my first month of note taking I discovered that I could have made $750 net income. I was working two jobs at the time and that certainly raised my eyebrows.

WHAT'S YOUR MOTIVE

Through this discovery I found one of the most important parts of this business. I found my motive. Ask yourself what's your motive. Why are you starting this business? Of course for income but be more specific. Maybe you want income to pay bills or take a family vacation.

Whatever makes you go after success is your motive. In order to work hard and be successful at something you've got to know why and how it can benefit you. For me working two jobs was not fun at all, and when I saw that I missed $750, it motivated me to get better. To get better all I needed to do was be more organized. This is a business and you must have the mindset to get organized. So I made a few adjustments on how I approached online auctions.

The first problem I had to solve was keeping track of auction dates and times. I started my online business before smart phones were all that smart lol. So I'd write the dates and times down and set the alarm clock or if I was at work I'd repeat the time over and over in my head so I wouldn't forget. I noticed that being online ahead of time gave me several advantages, which I'll touch on soon.

Another adjustment was calculating shipping cost, taxes, fees, so I would know exactly how much to bid and what would be the likely profit margin. Research is the most critical part of determining the financial success of your Internet auction business. So my goal was to hit $750 profit in the next month. I ended up making about $450 net. I won two auctions that consisted of used cameras. Even though I missed the mark it really felt great to earn that much online. I've never stopped buying ever since. The joy I felt from earning my own income was absolutely amazing to me and it's still just as exciting today.

The point is that if I didn't get myself organized. I wouldn't have made any profit and I can't imagine me still working two jobs to make ends meet. Take your auction business very seriously, it can be the difference in someone who earns a sale every now and then or a person who thrives online and lives the Internet lifestyle.

PLACES TO FIND PRODUCTS FOR SALE

While this course the design to teach you online strategies for auctions. I'd like to share with you some offline places you can find good items to sell online. I started selling on ebay back in 2007. At the time I didn't know about any of the online websites that sell items for cents on the dollar. I actually got my start buying products working for LOWES home improvement. We were having a store wide clearance sale and I needed some items for my home. In the kitchen and bath department I saw 20 kitchen faucets on clearance.

We needed a faucet for the kitchen at home so I asked the manager how much could I get one for including my Lowes employee discount. He went to the computer and said the faucet was regular priced at 29.99. They were on clearance at 50% off plus a 10% employee discount. I was pretty happy but then he said well today is your lucky day because these faucet are now considered non-stock items that the store would not be selling anymore. He was able to give me additional 10% off. The total came out to $9.73 for one faucet! Ding the light bulb came on, and I told him I'll take all 20 of them. I paid a little less than 200 bucks. Ebay was running commercial ads at the time so I signed up and sold every single faucet for an average of 22 bucks per item. So from then on I'd buy up clearance items from Lowes and Home Depot then flip them for quick profits. You can ask to speak to the department manager of any hardware or home improvement store and get a list of items that will be on clearance and non stock. This is a great way to get new products that people are looking for online.

I got even more determined as my income was starting to grow and I started looking for more places to buy items for cheap. I never know how much I would love the

Goodwill Thrift store until my laptop battery adapter went out and a friend mentioned to me that I could find a cheap adapter at a local Goodwill store. I walk in and thought to myself, this must be a dream! Not only did they have the adapter I was looking for, they had everything Electronics, Tools, Clothes, Furniture and more! The best part was that it was all cheap prices! I paid 5 bucks for the laptop adapter, which was about 35 bucks online. I've done really well with Thrift stores ever since then. The good news for you is that they still have everything for sale and it's still dirt cheap!

I'm sure you've heard of storage auctions and they are a really good way to get items cheap and make a profit. I've had really great lots and really bad ones. What you want to look for when bidding on storage auctions is location. If your at a storage auction in a poor area. Chances of finding nice items are slim to none. Look for upper class areas because there you'll find the gold! People in higher class areas of town normally put their old furniture and household items in storage and most of the time they end up buying new items and leaving the old stuff in storage. When you're at the storage auction make sure you get a good look before you bid. If it's crowded ask the auctioneer for time to view the lot.

Look at the condition of the boxes. Try to determine how long the items have been there or ask the auctioneers. Look for quality of the furniture. If you see solid oak wood, nice dresser drawers and lamps then you maybe looking at a winner. You can bet that if the furniture is nice then the items inside the boxes might have some value. Don't over bid! If you're facing stiff competition let it go unless you know the exact value of items you see. I've seen too many bidders get caught up in winning and not making a profit. My rule of investing, "If the bid is too high, say bye bye".

Other places to find items offline are estate sales. Now here you have an opportunity to win big. Estate sales are typically, items being sold because someone has passed away and the family wants to sell off the items and split the proceeds. Sometimes estate sale happen when someone has file for bankruptcy and the court orders the sale of home and belongings. You can Google estate sales and find several list to join for alerts in your area.

As the world of live auctions continue to grow you can find a unlimited supplies of live auctions. Google a list of registered auctioneer's in your state. Contact them or join their mailing list for upcoming dates. You'll find equipment, vehicles, electronics and more! It all about seeking the opportunity, there no limit on how much you can accomplish.

CHAPTER 2

HOW TO FIND PROFITABLE PRODUCTS ONLINE

You now have some general knowledge of how to set up your business and where to find some good products in your area. Now let's dive into the amazing world of online auctions. I can honestly tell you that online auctions have changed my life in so many ways. I'm honored to share this information with you. If you're like most sellers your main problem is finding enough good product to sell. Well my friend that's all about to end. In this chapter I'll provide you with the best places to buy items for cheap prices or cents on the dollar.

I'd like to share with you the first site that I found that was a complete eye opener for me. I was looking for a good used car, and I was on a limited budgeted at the time. I had about 1200 bucks to spend. I went to a local car auction and ended up with a lemon that I had to take back. Venting my frustration to my girl friend she offered up a website site she heard about from her job called public surplus. She mentioned one of her coworkers just bought a car for about 1,110 bucks and it ran really good. I admit I wasn't quite sold on the idea and I was thinking this must be another craigslist or something.

Despite my skepticism I went to www.publicsurplus.com to look for a car and Omg! I couldn't believe my eyes. All this time I had been finding products the hard way. Public Surplus is an asset liquidation company for government agencies. They sell all used or unwanted items from agencies that register with the government. These are public schools, colleges, city and state maintenance. On public surplus you can find just about anything. I ended up buying a ford Taurus from the city of corpus for only 565 bucks. It ran very good and I was happier than a rat in a cheese factory!

Naturally I spend hours and hours studying this website. I learned some tricks of the trade that I'll share with you now. Before you jump in, you'll need to pay close attention. All of the items are sold without warranty, meaning no refunds. Before you start bidding, read the entire description of an item. Don't bid on an item that's broken or needs extensive repairs, unless you are certain about all the cost to repair. Also pay close attention to the state the item is located in.

I would recommend buying in your own state before getting into purchasing in other state. (More on cross-state purchasing later) This way you can save time and money from shipping charges if you're able to pick up the item(s) on your own. Try to focus on buying lots. Lots are auctions that have 2 or more items for the price of one. You'll find that lots are three times more profitable than buying single item products. I started to Google and find other sites that sold surplus items and tripled my income! I'll share these with you now. After this chapter you'll have an unlimited supply of items to purchase. The good news is that these sites are always listing new surplus so you don't have to wait around for something good to pop up. If you get outbid for an auction there's always another good lot available so be patient.

WEBSITES THAT SELL ITEMS FOR CENTS ON THE DOLLAR

Before we get really deep into the specifics of bidding, I'm going to list all of the websites I currently used to build a highly successfully online business. I'll give my opinion on how they best benefitted me but depending on your selling niche you have a slightly different take from what you find.

1. Go-Dove.com A company that sells international goods and surplus. With this site I have found it to provide great medical and laboratory equipment. On occasion you might find some good cameras and audio/visual items. But the best part is the competition is not that high. This is because they typically list more than one of the same items so other bidders can purchase the same or similar item as you. The downside is shipping. Make sure you understand shipping and import cost before you bid. I'll be covering this topic in detail later in this course.

2. Govdeals.com is one of my personal favorites. A Government surplus management company with a huge selection of products in several categories. When it comes to finding a selling niche govdeals is king! Try not to get overwhelmed. I recommend browsing through all of the categories before you start bidding. If you have an area of expertise then go for it. If your new and don't quite know what to sell, then be patient. Add as many auctions to your watch list as you want and login at bidding time to watch the process.

3. Govliquidation.com is the number one site for military surplus. They have a wide selection of products no longer needed by the US military. You can find plenty of items here but you'll need to set you calendar as auction items are sold on monthly basis. For example most equipment is listed a month before the auction actually begins. The bidding process is normally 3-5 days. So for example and auction may be open for bids on the 8th but auction ends on the 11th. The good news is that govliquidation has the most lots of any other website so you'll almost always be purchasing more than one item. It's moderately competitive but if you've done your homework then you'll know how much to bid.

4. Gsaauctions.gov is a government owed website the list all types of assets. Buy real estate, vehicles, industrial sized equipment and more. They have been around a long time so competition is high but items are still selling way below market value. I found them to be a great source for communication equipment, medical equipment, and housing. Products are available for

purchase everyday and they offer really high dollar items. I've used this website to make big bucks. On the flip side you'll need a nice sized budget to compete. This is where I really begin to put partners together. Don't worry we have a section dedicated for partners later in the course.

5. Lonestaronline.com is a great auction site. If you are based out of Texas you will absolutely love this site. They sell seized and repo items as well as government surplus in Texas. So if you live or have relatives in Texas this can be a gold mine for you. I found this site to offer great vehicles for salvage and scrap, I've purchase huge lots of audio and video equipment and street maintenance equipment. The best part is that competition is really low. Even if you live somewhere other than Texas you can still afford to pay the shipping charges and make a nice profit. You won't believe how cheap the lots go for. The downside is that inventory is not as plentiful as other sites. You'll want to check it daily for new listings.

6. Proxibid.com is revolutionary in the live auction era. This website integrates online auctions and live offline auctions seamlessly. Make sure your Internet connection is good when bidding on the live auction. A live online auction is when an auctioneer is selling items from a remote location. The items are sold to the highest bidder. So you can tune in and watch and bid on real time auctions going on from your laptop, computer or smartphone. They offer a wide variety of high end products and equipment. The auctions are announced online and have specific dates so you'll need to keep track. Depending on your niche there is not a lot of competition except for the industrial equipment and trucks.

7. Publicsurplus.com is my go to site. As I mentioned it was the first site that I made a nice profit on and inspired me to find the others. Public surplus offer a countless variety of products. They only offer government agency products some of which are in poor to fair condition. The best part is you can always find a profitable lot on this website any time of day or night. The only downside is in some niches you're going to be competing with businesses and not other individual sellers. I see this mainly in construction and industrial equipment.

8. Repocast.com is owned by an asset management company called Miedema. Repocast is a network of eight auction websites group into to one. I use repocast because you can search all 8 sites from one location to find products. These auctions are scheduled out a week ahead. They sell assets

from stores, government agencies, repossessed items and more! I found this site to be a steal of a deal. Low competition and high valued items. Although their inventory is limited I seen growth in that area over the past year or so. Most of the items are sold in the northeastern part of the US so be mindful of the shipping charges. Also read each auction carefully the Internet premiums can vary.

9. Shopgoodwill.com is the thrift store queen. Not only can you find great deals at any local goodwill store but online is even better! You get access to every single Goodwill store's inventory online. Super large inventory and cheap prices. Auctions are happening all the time. The competition is moderate and if you lose an auction don't worry there's usually plenty more product of the same or similar type. It's great way to find books, used electronics, music equipment and more. The best part is they will ship your items directly so once your win the bid your shipping charges are automatically include in you invoice. So the entire process takes place online.

CHOOSING YOUR NICHE

You may have already gone and visited the websites mentioned above and that's perfectly normal. If your new to selling online I strongly recommend that you read over the course a few times until your comfortable enough to bid. Before you bid on an auction you must know what you're getting into. That's means knowing who your customer is and why they need your products. You may not know where to start buying and that's ok. What I would advise is that you start with items you already know the value of.

My level of knowledge was audio and visual equipment so in my early investment days all I bought was cameras, camcorders, tripods and music equipment. I stayed in that niche for years before I felt comfortable enough to branch off. Remember knowing the value is most important part because you actually make money when you buy, not when you sell. Ill get into the specifics of find the value in the next section. But for now as you browse the website look for items you currently or have recently purchased. If you're a frequent clothing shopper then start by bidding on purses, shoes, and clothing and fashion accessories. It really doesn't matter because you will be buying at really cheap price and you can resale it for profit.

I taught a guy I used to work with sometime ago and his niche was heavy equipment parts and tools. We worked in a corporate setting but his dad was a diesel mechanic so he knew a lot about welding, engine parts and vehicles. He and his dad started buying engine parts to rebuild and resale for profit. I can't tell you how gratifying that was for me. Which one of the main reason I decided to write the course. I want everyone reading this to benefit and learn to make great investment choices.

When you selected a niche or area you feel confident in. Start to build up your watch list across all the sites I've given you. This is an important practice because you won't win every auction and you need to get yourself several chances to win. I try to find 5-8 lots per niche per website. That gives me about 45-72 lots to bid on. Yes, there really is that much product online. Be willing to spend the time it takes to find the items. That's what determines how much you can earn. This business will pay you as much attention as you pay it.

Sure it can get dull or boring before you start to really make money but trust me it's so worth it. After you make a few sales you'll be hooked like a bass fish I promise. Also set goals for how much income you would like to make per month. Now ask yourself will this niche allow me to hit my goal if I'm able to sell 4-5 items per month? If your selling shoe laces (I hope not) then you wouldn't want to set a goal of 5,000 a month with this niche unless you had them endorsed by a famous athlete.

Be realistic, earning 5,000 per month is totally something you can do but your products need to have the value to support your goals. I was lucky starting with audio/visual equipment because they have a wide range of prices from cheap to arm and a leg expensive. The point is to be conscious of your niche and how much that niche can make per month.

So once you have built up your watch list full of items that you are familiar with it's time to bid right? Wrong, remember you can't become a successful online seller without knowing the value of the items you bid on. So let's get into the nuts and bolts of knowing the value of any product.

KNOWING THE VALUE OF YOUR PRODUCTS

I want to express how important this section is. Imagine buying a lot for say 500 bucks and your all excited because you picked the items you were familiar with. When the package arrives you open the box and begin to go through the items. All of a sudden it's not turning out the way expected. With every item you start to wonder what in the heck you were thinking about when you paid 500 bucks plus shipping. Well I hope that never happens to you but I've done it before. I figured out how to determine the value of what I was buying because I wanted to know exactly how much I should make before I bid on anything.

Remember, you make money as an online seller when you buy not when you sell. It's all about the research and now I want to share with you a few research strategies that have proven to make astounding profit margins. In my early investment stage I was fixated on audio/visual products because that's what I was familiar with. I bought a lot off of gsaauctions.com. It was a lot of video tripods. Gsa has highend products but you need a nice budget to compete. I had built up my savings and I was ready. The lot consisted of (2) Vinten Vision 12-SD tripods (3) Manfrotto 501 tripods (1) Miller DS-10 tripod and (1) Miller DS-25 tripod.

The first thing I did was google each of the model numbers to find out the retail prices online. I found listings from several websites and I took the prices from ebay, amazon, kitmondo, and broadcaststore.com. After comparing prices, I calculated the median price point. This is the average price an item currently is selling for online. Now let's do the math. The vinten 12 tripods were worth around 1,100 a piece at the time. The manfrotto tripods were about 700 a piece and the Miller DS-10 around 800 and the Miller DS-25 about 1,600 buck. So that meant that the lot was worth about 6,700 dollars. So now I was ready to set my budget and bid. Remember thinking there's no way I'm going to win but I'll give it a shot! 6,700 bucks wow and my budget was 2500 max! Meaning that would be the absolute highest I could bid because I still needed to pay for shipping. Thankfully there are no Internet premiums on GSA and no sales tax! So all I had to do was estimate the shipping based on the size and weight of the lot.

The idea is to get as much information about the lot as possible. I emailed someone on staff to find out an estimate on the weight of the items combined and also to clarify some of the model numbers that were not visible on the photo's and wasn't mentioned in the description. Making this contact turned out to be the best thing I could've done in securing the lot.

I ended up winning the lot for 1,869 dollars! I was so excited and happy I won, honestly I'm still happy about that lot because my online investing business really heated up after I sold those items on ebay. I tell that story because I learned so much with that lot and the money I made allowed me to buy several thousands of dollars worth of equipment that year. The shipping cost was around 350 bucks. So total invest was around 2,250.00 and I grossed about 6,200.00 with a net profit of around 3,080 bucks!

This was just one lot and the reason I believe I won was because I took the time to find out more information than my competition did. They couldn't have known the true value of the lot otherwise I would have been outbid. So make a mental note to go the extra mile and find out the most information. On every listing you find contact information from the sellers above the description. It could be the difference from you or someone else winning the bid.

So once you find a lot or item to purchase get the specifics on what the median price is. Factor in your shipping cost, Internet premiums and taxes if they apply. Once you have the best estimate value then you can bid with confidence and set your own goal for profit margin.

IS YOUR PRODUCT IN DEMAND?

Once you get things going it's really fun to do the research! I spend about 5 hours online everyday searching for profit. The next step in building a successful online auction business is finding products that are in demand. In this section we'll discuss some simple ways you can find the demand for your niche or product. Often sellers make the mistake of purchasing lots with high profit margins but are just simply not in demand. The worst thing is to buy a lot for a decent price and when you put your items up for sale know one buys or even watch your listing. You should know if people are in need of your product. One easy way to find out is to use ebay as a reference point of how many people are interested in a particular item.

For example lets take a Canon Gl2 camcorder. If you purchased this item you already know the fair market value online using the technique mentioned above. Now let's take it a step further. Type the name and model number of the item into the search bar of ebay.com. When you get your results, scroll down each listing. Get your note pad of open your notepad and write down the total amount of watchers you see from every listing you find with the Canon Gl2. I usually do this for the 1st and 2nd page of search results. Now add them up and you have a demand list. I will not invest in an item unless I can find 10 or more watchers for an item. Using this simple strategy has increased my profit margin and my buying power. There is absolutely no reason to fail! You are able to find the value and know how many people actually are interested in the item! I'm very proud to share this information with you. If I had known this when I started I could have made tens of thousands more! Thankfully you get to use it right away!

The other side of product demand is product saturation. You can run into big trouble if you purchase items that are highly saturated. The chance of your item being sold is less because there are more products than people watching the items. Be careful not to invest this way. You can have an item that you bought for say 50 bucks and the value is 250 bucks and your looking to make a 150 dollars profit. You have followed the steps for research but you don't do a saturation check. This can prolong your sale and force you to price the item lower than the fair market value to sell it faster. If you do this by choice then that is ok but the point is to know what you're doing when you buy.

The best situation would be a limited amount of items listed on ebay and several watchers on all the listings. When I see this I get very excited to buy because I know the item won't take very long to sell if I price it correctly. Remember I said finding out everything you can about an item(s) is key? Well here's another reason why. I bought some photography equipment from a Florida police dept on public surplus. In the description the item was not supported by the manufactor any longer. Item was a betterlight forensic kit but the software was dated and the company was now supporting a newer version.

This was an extremely high profit lot and I wanted it bad. I called the company because I wanted to know how I could get support or if there was an alternative route. They informed me that they were no longer supporting the version for business. I asked them if I have a problem or if the item needed repairs could I send it in. The guy said yes will take a look at it or recommend a authorized repair shop near you. Now this was the edge. On ebay the were only three of these listed and each listing had over 20 watchers, so the demand and saturation was perfect! The market range of this one item was 7,000-12,000 depending on if you had all the cables and accessories or not. The lot I was researching didn't come with all the bells and whistles so I knew I'd be looking to sell for 7,000-9,000 for the main unit alone.

I was a nervous wreck all day along I couldn't stop logging in to see if someone had increase the bid. (More on bidding later in this course) I knew I wanted to make a 3,000 profit or more so my max bid was 3,800. I made a phone call to the sellers on public surplus and asked them was the item working when they last used it. I was told the item was hardly ever used and they were selling it because they were going with another system for their lab testing. Now here was another edge. This gave me the ability to bid with confidence. I won the lot for 3,200 and I knew I was in for a big payday soon. You can use these same techniques and make big profits by knowing more than your competition. You see it's not that I had the most money in the world but I can guarantee you know one else knew as much information as I did a lot the item and it's current demand. I sold this item for 7,500 dollars in less than two weeks after I listed it. When you earn a payday like that it feels really good! It makes all the long hours you spend online worth it! The good news for you is that items like this example are still out there and you can buy them. If you do your research you'll know how much to bid and how much profit is on the table. I would love for everyone reading to make huge profits.

The truth is making a lot of money online is just like working a lot of hours on a job. Be proactive in finding out the details for the sellers when you're seeking information from them. It could be the reason you win or lose an important auction. I think it time we get into the action of online bidding. We'll discuss tips and strategies that beat out your competitors and you win!

CHAPTER 3

HOW TO BID LIKE A PRO

You've been building up your watch list and your demand research is on target. You've gotten all the information you could from the sellers and now you're ready to bid. That's great but before you start, I want to give you some tricks of the trade that will help you gain and advantage.

When you're getting ready to bid, try to be somewhere you won't be interrupted. A nice quiet place will help you stay focused on the auction. Organization is key. You may have several auctions ending on the same day or close to the same time. I open a tab for each website that I'm bidding on and as a backup I open a different browser with the same tabs in case I need to bid on the same site but a different auction ending around the same time as another auction I want to bid on.

Login to all of your accounts where you're bidding and do a check of your watch list. Look for recent bids in the bid history and see who was the first bid. You may not know who these people are but you want to get an idea of how many bidders you are up against. This information will help you understand what to expect once the auction is close to ending. If there are 6 bids on an items but only 2 user names then you know there maybe at least 2 or more bidders waiting for the end of the auction. In my experience there are typically two times of bidding processes. The first and most common is the time extension bid process. This is when an auction is below 5 minutes or less, the time will extend each time a bid is place. The time extension is generally 2-5 minutes.

This is done to allow the auction to sell to the highest bidder. The other type of auction bid process is the time run off bid. This type of auction has a countdown for the end time and will take the highest bid at the time it closes. You can set what's called a max bid for every auction you're bidding for. Be careful you don't set this max bid too early as it can give your competition an idea of your total budget. So let's discuss the right time to bid.

KNOWING WHEN TO BID

I never like to bid on an auction lot prior to 4-5 minutes until the auction end time. If you do bid before the auction end time your just driving the cost up and allowing your competitor to get a read on your bid patterns. I simple don't recommend bidding at all until the last 4-5 minutes left before the auction closes. Let's say you are on one of the more common bidding types and there is a time extension for the lot you're bidding for. You'll want to start with a minimum bid to see if that puts you in the lead. If it does then that's a good sign and your goal is to keep the lead until you win the auction or until you reached your max bid.

 Remember don't get caught up in trying to win. Your there to make a profit so, If the bid is too high say bye bye. You need to be very disciplined because if your not you'll end up buying lots where you may make a small profit, break even or actually lose money. So now you've gotten the lead you'll want to keep refreshing your bid history to check if other bidders are trying to catch you. Let's say you bid 75 bucks and you have the lead at 35 bucks. That's mean 75 bucks is your max bid for now. You refresh the bid history and you see a bidder has placed a bid for 55 bucks. Your still in the lead but the bidder is making a move for the lead.

What you want to notice is the bidder's pattern, the bidder make a bid 20 bucks higher than the current bid. Naturally you can expect the next bid to be 75 dollars or higher. When this happens it's time to rebid. Place another bid before your competitor can catch you. As soon as you see the bidder moving up place a bid for 95 bucks. Why is this important? Well for one the highest bidder gets the prize, but more importantly the bidder that's chasing you will begin to feel a defeated if every time they bid they see a message the read " you have been out bid please try again". You do this until you've reached your max and if you get outbid, don't sweat it move on to the next auction.

The other type of auction is what I call the count down. This is when there is no time extension and the auction will be over the second of the auction end time. Govdeals and shopgoodwill.com are the main sites that use this type of auction. I can tell you that it can be very frustrating and also very rewarding depending on if you win or not. In this case the auction still will sell to the highest bidder, but you wont have time to study bid patterns. You must have a fast Internet connection because with these auctions all the action takes place in the last 30 seconds. It 's very intense to say the least. You'll still want to be online 30 minutes prior and study the bid history from the time the auction began. Take note of how many bidders are there. What is the amount per bid? Are they bidding in 50 dollar increments or 100 dollar increments.

This will give you an idea of how much to bid down the stretch. What I do is wait about 1 minute before auction end time and place a bid for half of my max bid to see if I get the highest bidder lead. If so then I continue to refresh the auction if you get outbid that's ok take note of how much the highest bid is currently. Keep refreshing the page and if your max bid hasn't been surpassed then place the max bid with about 5 seconds remaining. Sometimes it can be a crap shot but most of the time this strategy works for me. You may need a few times to practice before you get the timing down. If you lose a couple lots this way don't give up Govdeals has plenty of auctions and plenty of profit.

COMMON BIDDING ERRORS

I want to share some of my bidding errors that cost me auction lots I should have won. It started to bother me when I'd lose an auction because of something other than getting out bid. So I'll share them with you in the hopes that you won't make these silly mistakes (lol). When I first started out bidding online I was very unorganized and I relied on my memory to recall the days I had auctions. This is huge mistake. Not because you can't remember but life is going to distract you and if you don't have reminders in place you will miss some auctions. There's nothing more sickening than when you miss an auction and you login to see what it sold for and it was rock bottom cheap. One time I miss an auction for 5 Nikon camera lens I can't remember the model numbers but the lot was worth about 1200 bucks. When I finally remembered in my mind about the auction I was two hours late and the lot sold for 185 bucks. I was sick to my stomach for days. Matter of fact I still lose sleep over that one.

Some auction websites will require you to place a deposit before you are allowed to bid. Make sure you check the listing description for this requirement. Mainly this is used for high dollar amount items. You'll need to make sure the credit card you have on file has enough money to cover the deposit. Yes, I have lost out like this as well. I didn't want my main debit card on file so I used a prepaid visa card and forgot I have spent the money on it. When it came time to bid, I was scrambling to replace the card info in my profile account, and by the time I entered the new information and submitted it. I got a noticed saying "Thank you for registering your credit card on file, verification may take up to 3-5 business days" OMG I lost out, I couldn't even bid so sad.

If you thought that was crazy I lost an auction once because I didn't read the auction end time correctly. It was an auction set for 6 pm Eastern time and I was in Central Standard Time. So I was thinking ok I get off work at 5pm it takes me 30 minutes to get home. I can be at home and ready for the auction with 30 minutes to spare. Sure enough I got home at 530pm turned on my laptop and realized I was off an entire hour! I could have bid from work had I gotten the time right. So check the time zones for each auction and set your alerts accordingly.

Keep a phone charger in the car at all times! I was on the road and I got an email alert for an auction ending soon. Just so happens I was driving through a country town in Texas at the time. My phone was on red alert with 3% remaining. My laptop was in the back seat but I was nowhere near an Internet connection. So I thought ok I've got 20 minutes. I can find a gas station and get a charge and bid from my phone. So I powered off my phone to save the energy and I'll be dam, I must have been on the longest oneway country road in America. When I finally got to a gas station, they didn't have any smart phone chargers. Sometimes it's just not meant to happen.

Don't forget about the shipping cost, Internet premiums and taxes. Before you dive all in with your max bid be sure you have estimated the bid plus all the others cost along with it. You can quickly lose money on an auction if you don't calculate this correctly. Shipping is the most uncertain cost so do the research before hand you can get estimate from any UPS, Fedex or go to USPS.com. They are extremely important when buying lots out of your area. You can contact them before you bid to find out if they will pick up your items and ship them to you.

Gather the zipcode of the auction location. Then visit UPS.com to find the nearest UPS store. Call them and explain to them that you may need some items picked and shipped to you. Most of the time they are willing to do this for a small fee of 25-35 dollars plus your shipping charge. If you can't locate a shipping company to pick the items up then you can contact a local courier service and have them bring the items to the closest UPS or Fedex store. If you stay organized then you should be well ahead of any common mistakes. There is a time when bidding you might be willing to bend the rules a little bit and go for the gold!

WHEN TO GO FOR THE GOLD

In the previous section you learned how to carefully calculate your auction. You should know exactly what the lot is worth plus shipping, taxes and fees. Sometime you may come across an auction where the seller is selling a huge inventory at once. In this case the description will not list all of the items that are included and often times if you call the person selling the inventory will not have a complete list. The lot is so large that Shipping through Ups or Fedex is not an option. What to do now? Use your best judgment and do research on all the items you can identify. Calculate how far of a drive it will be if you went and picked up the items yourself. Ask for additional pictures of the lot. I recently won an auction where a college film/television department was closing their program completely. They were selling everything from cameras, tripods, broadcast mixers, speakers, lighting equipment and a lot more.

The listing only described the model numbers for the tripods and a few cameras. The photos revealed a lot more than what the listing said. So I called and confirmed that everything in the photo's was included in the lot. I did some demand search on the tripods and camera's and saw that they were very high end and in demand on ebay. I got them to send me additional pictures and I was able to reach about 60% on the inventory. So that's what I based my max bid on. At 60% I had the lot worth over 20 thousand dollars and I won it for 6500 bucks. I had to rent a uhaul truck to bring the items to my storage and that was an extra 700 bucks. But I wasn't worried about that because I was still so for in the profit it didn't matter at all so I went for the gold! We spent enough time on buying, and I hope you have gotten a solid buying foundation. Now let's get to the money. It's all about selling what you've bought for big profits.

CHAPTER 4

LISTING YOUR ITEMS FOR SALE

I want to thank you for giving me the opportunity to share with you all of my buying and bidding techniques. Now that you have the hard part down, here comes the fun and exciting part of this business that never get's old! I'm talking about selling! If you love to sell things I hope you'll enjoy this chapter. Like I mentioned before the money is actually made when you buy not when you sell. However, in order to find a buyer and collect the funds you need to be able to list the item(s) for sale! So the question many people ask is where should I sale my stuff. Below I'll list some of the best places to sell online along with a brief description and my opinion of what the plus and minus of them are.

1. Amazon.com is a online market place for digital and physical goods. Excellent source for ebooks ,music, electronics and more! You can sell on amazon but it will cost you a fee for the seller account. They have a free seller account but it's extremely limiting because you can't list product that are not already in the database. Amazon has millions of visitors per month and you can sell pretty fast. The downside is that you make be required to enter a boatload of product inventory information if your product is not listed. The backend is a little confusing at first but you get use to it. You can typically charge about 3-5% more on amazon than ebay or other selling sites.

2. Ebay.com is an online selling platform where you can sell anything. High traffic and a frequent user base. Easy to list and supports every niche. Ebay has high final value fees and along with Paypal fees. The lower priced item usually sells faster and the competition is saturated depending on what you sell. Good for electronics, fashion and more! Be careful about your feedback score, Ebay will limit your accounts if you have too many negative feedback from customers.

3. Craiglist.org is an online classified ad site. You can list and sell just about anything here. There is no monthly or final value fee on craigslist. You pay for each listing individually. If you're into selling vehicles this is a great place to buy and sell. With no payment system, you must be careful not to be scammed. Don't meet up alone or go to anyone home to complete the sale. Try to arrange a meeting place in a public area, like at shopping mall parking lot. Check the cash and make sure it's not counterfeited. Other than that it's a great place to get leads and sell like crazy.

4. Shopify.com is a online shopping mall owed by yahoo. Great for fashion and accessories and electronic devices. No transaction fee, however there is a monthly subscription fee based on the plan you select. You can manage sells online and offline with shopify credit card payment system. You can build a custom online retail store using shopify for easy professional look. Down side

is that if you don't new products or clothing your sales may not be that great online and you'll need to focus on offline sales.

5. Equipmentone.com is an equipment and transportation market place. The website is owned by Richie Bro's Auctioneers. They are on of the largest auction companies in the world. Equipment one is quickly becoming the go to place for buying and selling everything from tractor trucks to heavy construction vehicles and more. Only a 50 listing fee, high traffic and small final value fee. An account rep will be assigned to your listing and you'll need proof of title before you can actually sell.

6. Saibids.com is a online selling site that features used electronics, cars, and government surplus. They are fairly new but quickly becoming one of the favorite sites to sell on as an alternative to ebay. All items are sold as is on saibids. I found this to be a great niche for selling with no worries of returns or negative feedback. The listing fees are cheap and the final value fees are lower than ebay or amazon. Not as advanced software as ebay or amazon and the price points are lower since everything is sold as is. Your account will need to be approved by staff before it is activated. You can choose from several online payment processors like Paypal, Authorize.net, and Skrill. If your selling used items this is a good place to sell.

7. Kitmondo.com is a large online market place for selling used medical, computers, broadcast and industrial equipment. Huge inventory of products. Easy listing features and a fraud prove buying and selling system. When you sell on this site you have to be patient. They will not release the funds until the customer has received the item(s) and give a feedback. Great place to list high end equipment in bulk.

8. Esty is a online market place for your hand made or self made products. If you're an artist you can sell your paintings here. Great for collectibles and organic items as well. More of a do it yourself site. If your item is not a highly sought after product you may have to bring your own traffic. They provide good information on how to promote your listing and seo strategies. Very trendy so be prepared to list and promote. If your item starts to buzz you can earn a lot. Great software and mobile apps.

There are more places to sell online, these are just the best places I found. No matter where you sell online the most important part will be how well you list and describe your items. In the next section I'll cover some tips on writing and creating listings that help you sell faster.

HOW TO WRITE EXCELLENT LISTINGS

Your first impression is often a lasting one, so you'll want to make a good impression online. You do this by creating a profile that clearly represents your niche. Many sellers fall short on sales because they don't represent themselves properly. When you register for any online market place, you have the opportunity to represent your business by entering information about your company. Make sure you write down in your profile your experience in your niche and why you provide the items for sale.

If you're an individual seller, I would recommend you still be as professional as possible. People want to buy from trusted sources and until you have enough feedback your profile will be all you have to let shoppers know who you are and why they should trust you.

Add a picture or logo to your profile. Give customers a visual feel of you or your business. If you don't have a logo you can get on upwork.com and have a designer make you one for 5-20 bucks. A logo way definitely separate you from the rest of the crowd so I suggest you get one done if you don't have a logo already.

Selling online is a skill. Many people think you can just toss a few pictures and a one sentence description and people are going to buy your items. I'm sorry but it doesn't work that way. In order to establish your self as an online business you must be willing to give your customers all the information they need to feel confident enough to purchase from you. The first thing a customer is going to want to look at is the description of an item. The description is your written guarantee of the current condition of an item. You must be as honest and descriptive as possible.

Think about each listing as if you were buying it. Wouldn't you want to know everything about something you were going to purchase? This is especially important for used items. Don't ever cheat a customer by not providing them with an accurate description. Nothing burns me up more than buying something online and when it arrives it's not at all like the listing described. I'll bad feedback them immediately and your customers will do the same if your not honest. If you're selling a used item you bought from government surplus, be sure to test it thoroughly. If you can't test or determine if the products works properly then list it for parts or sold as is. This way the customers can prepare to repair the item on their own expense.

When you describe an item, give the physical condition and the functional condition. An item can be in very good physical condition and not work at all. Obviously that's important to know. Don't reply on pictures to do all the work. On the other hand an item can have significant physical signs of use but function well. If your item has an expiration date of limited time of use make that known to the potential buyer. For example, if you're selling flowers or editable arrangements the buyer will need to know how long the items are good for use. This would be a major factor for the buyer decision and providing good solid information will give you and advantage over your competitors. It's also a good idea when selling used items to state were the item originally came from, especially for surplus items. You don't need to tell them you bought it from a surplus website but you can say something like.

"The Item was purchased from a local public school. The item is in working condition but has normal signs of use". This will give the customer some information about the item and help them make a buying decision. In most cases people like buying from schools. Items are typically still functioning and they are selling because of new inventory.

Selling new items are a lot less complicated but you still need to be descriptive. With new items make sure you have the specifications of the item inside your listing where they can be found easily. If you are an authorized retailer of the item make sure you state that in your listing. If you're only selling one type of item then start establishing yourself as an authority or expert and provide links back to your website if possible. You want your customers to know that you specialize in only this type of item. This will give you an advantage over your competitors. One of the most important aspects of new and used items are photo's. Without a visual a customer will find very difficult to purchase.

ADDING VISUALS TO YOUR LISTING

You've got your description down and now it's time to add the visuals. This is always the fun part for me because all of the hard work is done and I can't wait to show off my item. I want to share with you the importance of taking really good photo's and video of your items. You can lose out on so many sells because your pictures are crappy.

When I first started selling online, the quality of smartphone cameras was not all that great. I had to used a digital camera then transfer the pictures to my laptop. My first 20 or so listings didn't have great photo quality at all. I got beat out by sellers who were selling the same item even though my price was lower.

I was starting to wonder if I could compete with these guys. Then in a quest to get better, I studied their profiles and watched their listings. I noticed they had better and more detailed descriptions and higher quality photos. Sometimes making a few adjustments can make all the difference in the world! I notice that the top sellers never took photos of an item in their home. Well it could have been from their home but you would never know it.

Before you take a single photo of an item, get yourself a plain white background. This can be white paper, a white tarp or cloth. Hang it up in your garage or a wall in your home or office space. Make sure it is clean and doesn't have any spots on it. Next grab a lamp or if you have it, some photography lighting equipment and light up the white background. Now place the item in front of the background and take the photo. Simple yet so many sellers use unprofessional pictures and their items sit and don't sell.

Professional pictures don't require a professional camera. Any decent smart phone camera will work so long as the item is highly visible and well lit on a white background. If you move while taking a photo and it's blurry, erase it and start over. Don't upload fuzzy or blurry pictures, it shows that you are lazy and don't really care about what your doing. Remember your customers are smart buyers, don't give them any reason to choose someone else.

A new trend is starting in online selling. That is the use of video. Video provides and addition source of visual proof on condition. Video is a great tool for selling items that require proof of functionality such as vehicles. You can get a lot of mileage of video in your listing. Make sure the site you sell on allows video. Most will allow a Youtube format with a short link or embedded code. Keep the video very short and to the point of showing the function.

If selling a vehicle then start the video before you crank the engine or motor. Adjust the sound so that the video is not too loud and distracting. Video is a good way to explain features or a defect that customers can see and understand. I'm an advocate for selling with video and hope you use it more as well. So after you have created a detailed and informative description, and uploaded clean well taken photos and/or video, it's time to price your item.

HOW TO FIND THE PRICE POINT

In order to collect on all the hard work it takes you need to have the right price. Don't worry it's pretty easy to find out what you should be charging but research is the key. Remember all that research you did to find out if you should buy the item?

Here's where you'll be glad to know that you have already done have the work in finding the right price point. You should have some idea of what the item(s) or worth. Finding the right price point is about sizing up your competitors and giving customers a reason to choose you over them.

Price point are relative to the website you are selling on. So you want to check all the listings of sellers that are selling the exact item(s) you are selling. What you are looking for is any advantage you can find. For example if your item is in better condition you have an advantage. If you item is in worst condition you still need to know because that will help you price the item appropriately.

Let's say you have an iphone 5 for sale and you research and find 10 other sellers with the same item in used condition. The average median is 199.99 but you noticed some have sold for 350 dollars. Take notice of the condition. It may have sold for more because the item was only used once or twice with no marks or scratch. It could be because the phone is unlocked and will work on all major phone carriers. Try to study listings and know why a similar item will sell for more or less and than your item. Knowing this will definitely help you sell faster!

Be careful not to under price your items. Many sellers have cut themselves short on profit because they price far below the average median. I recommend you don't do that. The main reason is because you're driving the value of all the items down. It's like living in a well kept neighborhood and someone moves in and leaves trash all over the front lawn. The trash ends up on your lawn and you have an appraiser coming to inspect the area. Thanks to this guy your home is now worth less. Stay close to the median price point unless you have a reason to price below such as a defect or your selling the item for parts only.

Shipping plays a huge role in how I price my items. If you're dealing with items that can be boxed and shipped by UPS or Fedex here's a neat trick that works well. Find out what the weight of your item(s) is. You can use a bathroom scale or reference the box the items came in if you shipped them to yourself. Contact a shipping provider and do a couple shipping quotes. For example if you live in New York ask them for a shipping quote to deliver your item to a city in California. Try to figure the cost of the furthest distance in your country.

This is will give you a great price reference for how much to charge for shipping in your listing. Now here comes the trick, If your item can be boxed and you know the estimated cost of shipping. Offer free shipping in your listing. That's right, offer free shipping to your customers and add the cost of shipping on the price of sell. Customers love free shipping! This will give you a huge advantage over your competition. As a buyer you just want to pay one time and be done the purchase and many time you can lose a sale because the shipping is to high! Shipping is a big deal and well cover how to get the most bang for your buck in the next section.

CHAPTER 5

GETTING YOUR PRODUCT TO THE CUSTOMER

By now you realize just how much work goes into to buying and selling online. You've bought and sold an item but you're not done yet. You must complete the transaction by getting the product safely to the customer. It seems like this should be the easiest part but it's not. I had really good sales go bad because of poor shipping techniques that I had to quickly correct. After you sell an item don't throw the item in a box with old newspaper and send it off. If you do you're asking for disaster. There are a few things to consider before you put the product out for delivery. If you are going to package and ship the item yourself you need to be extremely careful in choosing the box size and providing enough bubble wrap or peanuts. As a general rule you should measure the height length and width of your item. Make sure the box or package you use have at least 2 inches of space from the edge of the box or package.

For example is the item is 18x14x6 inches, then your box needs to be 20x16x8 or larger. The proper box size will help prevent items arriving damaged. Whenever you ship an item it has to be transported on and off a truck load full of other boxes and items. It is very important that you pad the box or package with peanuts or air bubble wraps. Don't assume the mail carrier is going to treat your package with special care. Truth is they are going to throw your box on and off the truck when handling it. For this reason you must consider the type of item you have and if it's consider to be fragile or not.

Cameras, lens, or any item with glass I always treat as fragile. Write fragile on the top bottom and sides of the box or package. This will alert the mail carrier that your item should not be thrown or stacked on by other boxes. Try to use bubble wrap on all your items. You can find a local shipping supply store in your area and buy the bubble wrap, peanuts and boxes in bulk. This will save you big bucks on shipping cost. You can even find a tape gun, fragile stickers and do not bend stickers for your items as well.

CHOOSING A SHIPPING COMPANY

If you don't want to bother with the hassle of packing an item you can just bring to a local shipping retailer such as FEDEX ,UPS or USPS. For smaller items I found the USPS to be the cheapest way to go. For large boxes you'll want to use UPS ground for the most affordable price. If you have an item in a package envelope or small box, try

Fedex they will get the package there quickly and a decent price. There are other benefits of choosing a shipping retailer to handle your items.

The main reason is you don't have to worry about shipping supplies or wondering if you did a good job of packing the item or not. You can save a lot of time by using a retailer. I like to use them because I can impress my customers by providing them with a tracking number the same day they purchase and pay for an item. Never ship an item without making sure you have received payment. In addition you can purchase insurance for the item in case it arrives damage you don't lose money on the sale.

If you are selling large items over three hundred pounds, then you want to have it transported on a truck. UPS freight handles large palletized item. You'll want to get your own pallets and shrink wrap the items before you call UPS freight to schedule a pick up. Have the approximate size and weight of the pallet for a quote over the phone. For vehicles, heavy equipment try getting a shipping quote via UShip.com Make sure you get the quote before you list the item. The customer may have their own shipping arrangements but you want to be able to offer them a shipping quote.

GET YOUR ITEMS INSURED

If the item you have sold is over 1000.00 in value, I recommend you have it insured. I know it can be a tedious extra charge but it can save you from financial set back. I sold a microscope once and I had it shipped via UPS freight. It was about 350 pounds. I got a pallet from the back of a home improvement store and bought the shrink wrap. I wanted to save on the shipping cost because the quotes I got were too expensive to prepare the pallet. The microscope was worth about 6,000 bucks. UPS freight would not insure the item because of the value. So I didn't have the item insured. I was confident in the job I did shrink wrapping the microscope.

The customer called me in out rage when the package was delivered. The top part had been broken off. I ended up having to file a damage claim in which UPS denied and I had to refund the customer a portion of the sale so he could buy the piece he needed to use the microscope. What a total disaster for me. I could go to an insure company and gotten trip insurance for the load and I would made an additional profit. Instead I got an angry customer, a denied damage claim and a loss on the total sale. Never again will I ship any item of high value without insuring it. Use your best judgment for insurance but if it's worth a lot to you then insure it. Better to be safe than sorry.

TRACKING YOUR PACKAGE

Tracking an item is a vital part of the entire shipping process. It is the last step but most important. Without a tracking number your items could be loss or unaccounted for. You especially want to get a tracking number when shipping internationally. You may find yourself tempted to ship USPS when you have a buyer from a different country. It's ok because they normally have a better price than UPS or Fedex but be sure to get tracking. I've lost a couple items this way. I was fixated on saving money on the shipping and the items got lost or delayed.

In one instance I shipped a watch overseas and I didn't get tracking. The package was lost for weeks and the customer demanded a refund. I of course had to honor the request. I did some calling around to see if the package had been found and finally I got someone who was willing to investigate and I discover that the package had been deliver to the customer a week prior. I was in outrage but when I contacted Ebay about the matter the first question I was asked was why didn't you track the package. I had to take the lost because I had no way to prove the customer actually got the package in hand. It may have been out for delivery but I couldn't prove without a doubt that it was delivered to the customer. When you ship internationally or domestically, be certain that the full address is visible and can be read easily. I lost another item because the zip code I wrote on the box was mistaken and the box ended being received by the wrong person. They never returned the box and I lost again. I hope you are taking note so you don't make these mistakes I did. It can cost a lot of money depending on what you've sold. There's nothing fun or exciting about taking a loss you don't need to take.

CHAPTER 6

PROVIDING GREAT CUSTOMER SERVICE

Selling is really exciting, especially after you have received payment and shipped the item(s) off to the customer. Time to move on to the next item right? No it's not. Being a good seller has several benefits. What determines if you're considered a good seller is your customer service. When a customer buys from you and get exactly what they expected is what makes the online market place so prominent and promising. You'll want to work hard at being a dependable and reliable seller. It will bring you repeat business and referrals so your income will increase once you establish a good customer service reputation online.

One of the first steps in building that trust in customer service is establishing direct contact with your customer. When you sell an item, make sure you contact the customer shortly after. You'll want to thank them for their business and provide tracking information or shipping details. Tell your buyer that you or your business is available via email or phone if support is needed at anytime. Right away your customer will start feeling good about the purchase they just made. When your item arrives give the customer a couple of days to observe the item(s). Normally if you don't hear from them then they are satisfied with the item.

I like to send follow up emails for three reasons. For starters you really gain the trust of a customer when you provide great products, communication and follow though. The second reason is to ask the customer to provide feedback or testimony. Feedback is the benchmark for how your potential customers perceive you as a seller. If you've gotten really good feedback, other customers will trust and by from you. Alternatively if your feedback is questionable then you will lose a lot of buyers to your competitors. The third is reason is once I have followed up with the customer and gotten a good feedback. I can now disburse funds and pay myself. That's right I recommend that you don't touch the money you collect from a sale until you know the customer is happy. No matter how hard to try to be perfect at selling you will experience an unhappy customer and when the transaction goes south you need to be able to refund the customer or provide a reasonable solution to the problem.

BE A PROBLEM SOLVER

When transactions don't go as smooth as you planned, be a problem solver. Your customer will contact you when they are not totally satisfied. Before you offer a refund, try to solve their problem. A good practice in selling and in life is to try to think about 5 ways to solve a problem when you have an issue. Act as if you are the customer and see if you can think of different ways to satisfy the customer while keeping the transaction in tact.

For example let's say you sold laptop and the customer writes you in an out rage because the laptop is working properly! You remembered you tested the laptop before you shipped it. The customer states that it doesn't work correctly and wants a refund. You can be a problem solver and offer several solutions that may make the customer satisfied. One solution would be to exchange the laptop, and send another one of the same or similar style. Make sure you have the customer return the original one sold.

Another solution would be to have the laptop evaluated by a local repair shop in their area and pay for the service. You could have the customer return the item and you inspect the item. If it is indeed not working you could fix the issue yourself and send it back. You offer a partial refund if the problem is minor and something the customer won't mind dealing with on their own. Lastly if all else fails and the customer is still insisting on a full refund don't hesitate to give them their money back. You can always relist the item and make another sell on it. Make sure you get the item back before you send the refund. Not all customers are honest.

DEALING WITH DISHONEST CUSTOMERS

As a rule I'd recommend you always state that the customer must pay for return shipping. I do this to avoid customers who buy items to use for a short period and want to return the item. I've seen other companies and sellers also charge a restocking fee. Unfortunately you'll have to deal with dishonest customers. As you become a more seasoned seller, you'll be able to detect fraudulent customers. Be careful for customers asking where you or your items are located. If you're doing large cash transactions, don't be afraid to let the customer know that you will need to verify cash and/or checks with your bank before you give title or possession of the item(s) or you could find yourself in a transaction with a customer that is trying to pull off an insurance scam or some type of refund scam. A common misuse of shipping is damage insurance. Remember the guy I mentioned when I sold him the microscope? I shipped it UPS ground and he filed a damage claim saying that the top part of the microscope was damaged during shipment. After UPS investigated they denied his claim and also denied my claim so I lost out because the package actually arrived in tact according to UPS and so they didn't award either of us.

I had already given the customer a partial refund and that was a big mistake. If you have any dispute with a customer don't offer a refund until the matter is completely resolved on both sides before you issue a refund of any type. Had UPS granted his claim he would've gotten the insurance money from UPS, which was equal to the value of the item, a partial refund from me and kept the microscope! Trust your instinct if a transaction doesn't feel right. Ask someone from your selling platform to help. I'm pleased to share with you that after nine years of buying and selling, the majority of your transactions will be good customers looking for great products!

GETTING REPEAT CUSTOMERS

One of the most rewarding parts of selling is having a customer come back and purchase from you again. Repeat customers are a good indicator that you are providing great customer service. If you have a niche business that requires a monthly or weekly purchase, then repeat customers are your bread and butter. If you sell for example, an organic soap or lotion, making sure you have repeat customers is the most important part of that business.

So how do you get customers to come back? It's all about great products and service. I'll share with you some techniques I use to get customers buying again. You must first lay a solid foundation for the customer to trust you. Use the techniques mentioned earlier in this chapter. When you make a sale follow up is one way you can get an idea of what the customers needs are.

Knowing what the customers needs are can help you make suggestions that can lead to more sales. Whenever you sell try to indentify the accessories that compliment the item or product. After you get good feedback from a customer invite them to visit your seller profile and see more of the items you have available.

Another great way to get repeat business is to become a wholesale resource of a particular niche. For example you may have a way to find very cheap digital picture frames. You could offer the item to seller for a discount if they buy in bulk from you. If you sell on Saibids, Ebay or Amazon you will have the customer email and address information after payment is processed. I recommend you create an email mailing list using customers that have already bought from you.

Ask the customer if it's ok for you to add them to your mailing list for future discounts and announcements of new products available. Let them know that you will not share or spam their inbox. Most of the time they will say yes, and this is the start of building a repeat customer relationship.

CHAPTER 7

EXPANDING YOUR BUSINESS

The most rewarding part of selling online is having the ability to expand your niche and create a full online business for yourself. Once you have established a niche online you can enjoy the feeling of making money and providing great customer service. If you're looking to sell online as your main source of income, you will need to expand your niche or choose new products to sell. It's all about variety when it comes to gaining more sales on a daily or weekly basis. You must build an inventory of products or equipment that people are looking to purchase. You're not going to sale enough with one niche to support a full time income. So you want to think of yourself as an online pawnshop.

The reason pawn shops stay in business is because they have a large selection of common products that people need or want. As you search the buying websites, looking for items that people are bidding on frequently. If your first niche is electronics, then start by expanding your electronics inventory. I started with cameras and camcorders, then I expanded to camera accessories like tripods and lens. After I got familiar with those, I expanded to audio and video production equipment. So you can see a pattern of choosing a niche and expanding on the accessories of that niche.

The research you do for your current niche will also help you choose another niche. The second niche I choose after electronics was heavy equipment and utility vehicles. I started watching sewer equipment and street maintenance vehicles. I was browsing and saw an auction ending of public surplus. It was a vacuum truck and the bid was around 25,000! I though to myself hmm, I wonder if I could find a similar vehicle on the other sites for less. Sure enough I was able to find several. I started building my watch list and studying the price point of each vehicle. I went to the websites for these vehicles and read information about their purpose. This helped me to understand what the demand was and why they are needed. After a couple months of research I felt confident enough to bid. On my very first vehicle I bought a vacuum truck for 15,100 on govdeals.com and sold it for 27,500 on equipmentone.com. I knew I had found a very good and profitable niche. I expanded the niche by investing in sewer equipment such as pipeline inspection and manhole cameras. I found out that all of these were relative to the street maintenance and utility truck industry. The exciting part was that every city and all over the world need these this type of equipment in order to keep sewers from becoming clogged and for keep the streets clean. So the demand is very high for this niche but you'll need to save up because the bidding price points are high.

As with any niche you decide on make sure you study before you start bidding. You should already know the profit margin before you bid. If you don't' know, that means you're not ready to bid and you need to continue your research. If you're just starting out investing online and don't have thousands of dollars to invest that's ok. There are plenty of niches that you can make thousands of dollars on investing only a couple hundred bucks or less. You can also make money with out spending a single dime of your own money. That's right once you become an authority in your niche another way to expand that niche is to sell other products through affiliate marketing programs.

AFFILIATE MARKETING PROGRAMS

Affiliate marketing is the online version of a business referral. This is when you the seller partners with a vendor and agree to a fixed commission for referring customers to the vendor. For example if you sell used cars as a niche and your website or selling platform brings in tons of traffic. You would want to partner with a dealership or someone else who sells cars to increase your revenue.

If you have a visitor that comes to your selling platform and clicks on a link or banner that takes them to your affiliates selling platform and make a purchase, you get a commission based on the sale amount. Just about every major selling platform will have an affiliate marketing program. It makes since for both the seller and vendor to partner and bring more traffic and customers.

Before you chose to market another product I recommend you know as much as you can about a particular niche. If you're good at selling electronics stick to that niche as an affiliate, you'll have a better chance of being a successful affiliate marketer. The common mistake people make is choosing to promote vendor products they know nothing about. They choose these niches because the commission may be high or frequently sold. However the chances of your customers trusting you in a different niche is rare. So be certain that your current niche support the niche that you are marketing from the affiliate program. Below I'll list a few affiliate marketing programs you may find useful to your niche.

1. Ebay.com has an ebay partner affiliate program. You get commissions based on converting traffic that you send to ebay.

2. Amazon.com has an affiliate program good for books and electronics

3. Clickbank.com is one of the worlds largest affiliate programs for digital products good for how to- ebooks and software.

4. Commission Junction is one of the largest online retail affiliate marketing programs, good for promoting major brands.

Each of these will require you have a selling platform of your own such as a website or blog. Read the terms and conditions before you apply and be certain that you have done the research the products you plan to promote. You may need to invest a small amount of money into ppc advertising or search engine submission for addition sales. I'll be covering more on this topic in another course. None the less affiliate marketing can be a great source of additional income if choosing a niche you are already familiar with and drive traffic to your vendors selling platform.

After you have two or more niches you may be ready to corner those niche and become a dominant presence online as an authority. If you are making profits on most of the purchases you make, it may be time to expand by increasing your buying power.

INCREASE YOUR BUYING POWER

You have taken a niche and expanded to more niches and you're ready to buy more and make more profits. This is really great and I'm glad you've made this far. I wouldn't recommend you borrow any money from a bank or private lender unless you have a proven track record of success in your niches. Online sales are not predictable so, you need to understand that borrowing money to increase power is a commitment you are willing to payback if you sale your items or not. Set a budget based on the sales you are already getting per month to determine how much to ask for. If your total gross sales are around 3-5 thousand a month then I would recommend you borrow 1500-2500 hundred for buying. Try to stay below your monthly gross sales to save room for the monthly payment of the loan take out from a bank or lender. You can find several sources to borrow from other than a bank or private lender. You can use a credit card for example or a business line of credit. Online shopping is growing at a record pace. Banks and lenders are starting to adapter and expand their lending services to online sellers like you and I. This wonderful news! In the near future you won't have to fill out an application to get funds for your business.

You will only submit your seller account information and provide basic business account information. Your lender will examine your transactions and give a loan based on your sales track record. The frontrunner for this type of lending is a company called Kabbage. You may have seen their advertisements online on sites like Ebay, Amazon or social media. I'm a current client and I use funds from my Kabbage.com account to make purchases each month. Look for more types of these companies to form as we get closer to 2020. The fact that you have developed a skill will attract business lenders to you.

If your credit score is not up to standard don't worry soon it won't be much of a determining factor in your ability to borrow for your online business. As an alternative you can borrow from yourself as a way to increase buying power. A neat technique you can use is to start a CD account with a local credit union. A CD is a certificate of deposit. For example if you have 2500 saved up and you want to borrow 2500 for purchasing. Go to the credit union and open a CD account. Put the 2500 in a savings account for a set term of 12months.

Then ask for a loan on the CD in which you will pay back on or before the mature date, which would be in 12 months. One benefit is that you get the cash right away to start buying. The second benefit is that you are establishing business credit with a lending institution. Once you pay the loan back the credit union will offer you an unsecured loan! Other source of expanding your business involves a more personal approach. You can recruit partners to invest in your business and increase buying power and profits.

CREATING PARTNERS

One of the most rewarding aspects of this business is creating good solid partnerships. It's a really good feeling to have the trust of someone who is willing to invest in your ability to find and deliver a profit. People form partnerships all the time but not all partnership are the same. Before you ask someone or accept a partnership offer, be certain that you have acquired enough expertise in your niche. You also want to be able to provide your proof of profit. Most of your selling sites will keep record of your sales for the past 90 days. It's a good idea to have an inventory list with purchase price and sale price to keep account of your net sales. Quickbooks is a software designed to help online and independent business owners track and manage inventory and sales. A great tool for your business portfolio as well. The main question I get about partner is how to find the right person or business to bring in.

The most common mistake I hear about in partnerships is when you choose a friend or family member as an investment partner. Try to avoid this if at all possible. Friends and family tend to have trouble removing emotions in the partnership. Sometimes you will need to make a business decision and if your partner is a friend or family member who is inexperienced you could end up damaging the relationship as well as the partnership. Sometimes you will need to make a business decision and if your partner is a friend or family member who is inexperienced you could end up damaging the relationship as well as the partnership.

There are only two types of partners that I consider. The first type is a silent partner. That means finding someone who has seen or believes in your ability to produce profits. A silent partner will not interfere with your buying decision and a fixed percentage is usually how the contract is written. Always have a written agreement with anyone you go into business with.

The percentage will be determined by how much the silent partner is willing to invest. For example let's say the investment is 10,000 and the profit will be 20,000. The silent partner is willing to invest 5,000. In this case the partner will get 40 percent of the profit plus the 5,000 he or she has invested. So would be 9000 for the silent partner and 11,000 for me.

If the silent partner is willing to invest the entire 10,000 then I would ask for 40% of the profit in which he would get 16,000 and I would get 4,000. Silent partners are not people who hand over their money and go away. They want to know how you plan to bring their income back and in what time frame you expect to deliver it. Always give yourself plenty of time to sell the inventory or equipment. If normally takes you 30 days to turn a profit tell your silent partner to give you 60 days. This will give you some time in case you run into unexpected challenges with the investment.

The other type of partnership I recommend is a seller 50/50 partnership. I only do 50/50 partnerships with other sellers who understand the business and can add value to the partnership. A 50/50 partner should have just as much or more knowledge as you in regards to making investments and turning a profit. This type of partnership I find to be the most rewarding. You never stop learning and seller partnerships are great for learning new niches! I have several seller partners that I deal with. One partner introduced me to buying and selling real estate. There is so much you can learn from other investors, it's a good idea to surround yourself with them and share your knowledge.

In closing I would like to thank you sincerely for reading this ebook! I thank you for your support and I certainly hope you have learned and will grow from this information. If you're just starting out with online investing, please read this ebook as often as needed. Remember your research is very important. You make money when you buy, not when you sell. I'm here for you contact me at membersonly@sellforaliving.com

My Very Best Regards

Carlton Richard

www.ingramcontent.com/pod-product-compliance
Lightning Source LLC
Chambersburg PA
CBHW070426190526
45169CB00003B/1426